WHAT THEY DON'T TEACH YOU ABOUT HISTORY

by **TIM WOOD**   illustrated by **IAN DICKS**

DERRYDALE

NEW YORK

To Charlotte and Laura, who could never be described as horrible historians.

Thanks to Rachel Wright, Morven Thomson and Iain Craig for their extra research.

Contents

Introduction

The world is divided into two types of people – those who enjoy history and those who don't. Usually the ones who do enjoy it had the good luck to be taught by a teacher who made the subject come alive for them. That teacher almost certainly had a seemingly inexhaustible supply of stories, with which to shock and excite his or her audience.

This book contains some of the more horrible stories in human history. Anyone who is easily shocked should read no further. Those of you who want to know more will be pleased to hear that this collection barely scratches the surface. There's lots more where these came from!

Of course, since the incidents in the book are the most grisly and horrible from our history, they should remain as past events. **Under no circumstances should you try to make this sort of history repeat itself!**

We must be careful when we look at the habits and customs of people who lived in different circumstances from our own. Beliefs and behavior were different then, and before we criticize we need to know more about the period. In any case we have no reason to feel smug and superior about our own performance. There is still a good deal of cruelty and unhappiness in the world. War, torture, slavery, and crime still exist. People still wear uncomfortable fashions and eat food which is very bad for them. We've a long way to go before we can pat ourselves on the back and congratulate ourselves for being truly civilized. If you are curious, read on . . .

6

Food and Drink

We all have to eat to live, and over the course of history people have eaten just about everything, including each other. Who knows how many people have died tasting new foods, trying out new recipes or even being new recipes? We have to admire the bravery of the very first person to eat a snake, a frog, or a snail. We should be very grateful to these early pioneers whose courageous experiments have taught us what is good to eat and how best to prepare it.

Most animals are eaten somewhere in the world. People enjoy horse, monkey, ants and grasshoppers. The rule seems to be if it moves, eat it.

Roman Rodents

The Ancient Romans were very fond of eating. There are tales of them stuffing themselves at feasts with a huge variety of dishes. One great delicacy was dormice. These were served in a huge variety of ways. It was said that dormouse experts would discuss their favorite food in very much the same way as wine connoisseurs talk about wines today.

Poison Potentate

Normally people avoid poisons. Not so King Mithradates VI of Pontus in Asia Minor. He was terrified of being assassinated, so he took small doses of poison to build up his resistance to it. Unfortunately, in 63 BC he wanted to kill himself to avoid being captured by the Romans. He took poison, but of course it had no effect. In the end he had to fall on his sword!

Sounds Fishy

Another great Roman delicacy was a drink made from the insides of various fish. These were salted and then exposed to the sun until they went rotten. The liquid was drained off and drunk.

Greedy Emperor

One of the largest eaters in Ancient Rome must have been the Emperor Maximian. He was said to eat 40 pounds of meat and to drink 9 gallons of wine every day. For exercise he would crush large stones with his bare hands. He reigned for nearly twenty years.

Malnourished Monarch

Another famous gargantuan eater was England's King, Henry VIII. Strangely enough historians now think that he died because of what he did *not* eat. Like most rich people in Tudor times, Henry ate huge amounts of meat and almost no vegetables. Vegetables were thought to be suitable only for the poor. Henry suffered from bleeding gums, leg ulcers, stomach pains, coughing and depression. These are all symptoms of scurvy, a disease caused by a lack of vitamin C.

After Dinner Puke

Eating tends to make you feel full. However, this was no problem to the Ancient Romans who wanted to carry on sampling the menu. They simply used a feather to tickle the back of their throat, vomited up everything they had just eaten, and then started all over again! Special rooms were sometimes set aside for the vomiters so they did not stop other people from eating! Seneca, a famous Roman writer, remarked that Romans "ate to vomit and vomited to eat". He criticized extravagant dishes such as pâté of song birds' tongues, stews of nightingales' livers, and dishes of parrots' heads, camels' heels, or elephants' trunks.

Chocoholic

The Aztecs' favorite drink was a kind of cold cocoa. It was made from the beans of the cacao tree which were flavored with vanilla and spices, whipped, allowed to dissolve gradually, then drunk cold. The Emperor Montezuma had 50 jars of this drink made every day for his personal consumption, and 2,000 jars for his household!

One Lump or Two ?

When tea was first introduced in the American colonies many housewives, unfamiliar with the correct method of making tea, served the leaves with sugar or syrup after throwing away the water in which they had been boiled.

Powerful Punch

One of the most exciting cocktails must have been the "Pirate Special" invented by Edward Teach. Teach, who was better known as the pirate captain Blackbeard, never washed. His clothes were stained with drink and blood. His favorite drink was rum mixed with gunpowder. Some say he used to light the gunpowder just before he tossed the drink down. No doubt he found it very warming on cold winter nights!

9

Ale and Hearty

Fashions in food have changed tremendously. Nowadays people are starting to recognize the dangers of alcohol. However, in 1632, a children's hospital in Norwich, England included 2½ gallons of beer in its weekly ration for each sick child.

Have a Drink on me

U.S. President, Rutherford Hayes, and his wife, who was known as "Lemonade Lucy," never consumed alcoholic beverages. During his term of office, Hayes banned any kind of alcohol from the White House. However, the butler was only too willing to help the parched guests – for a price. He spiked the sherbet punch with alcohol. Grateful visitors gave him large tips for his help. The President never discovered his butler's little business.

Let's Tuck In!

Eating habits have changed quite a lot in the last few hundred years. Here is a menu for a meal served to Henry VIII and 30 guests. 800 eggs, 90 dishes of butter, 50 loaves of chestnut bread, 300 wafers of marzipan, plus 6 apples, 7 pears and 10 oranges per person.

So much for the starters! The serious part of the meal consisted of roast beef, veal, lamb, capons, plovers, woodcock, partridges, herons, snipe, leverets and lambs' tongues. This was washed down with 2½ gallons of beer and wine per person! Henry had meals like this served almost every day. Not everything was necessarily eaten by the guests but Henry grew very fat with this continual feasting. His waistline increased by 16 inches in five years. He became so heavy that ropes and pulleys had to be used to haul him into his 13 foot-wide bed.

Nasty Nosh

The worst royal food in Britain was probably served at the court of Henry II. The meat was spoiled and putrid, and the wine so thick with dregs the courtiers had to filter it through their teeth.

Sing a Song of Sixpence

Charles I did not eat as much as Henry VIII, but he liked surprises. He was particularly fond of elaborate pies. One was baked for him which actually did contain the famous 24 live blackbirds.

Balanced Diet

Louis XIV was not such a greedy eater as Henry VIII. However, he didn't exactly go hungry. He often dined on a meal consisting of four plates of different kinds of soup, a whole pheasant and a whole partridge, chicken or duck, stuffed with truffles. This was accompanied by a huge quantity of salad, some mutton, two slices of good ham, a dish of pastry and some raw fruit, compôtes and preserves. At his post-mortem Louis was found to have a vast stomach, and bowels twice the usual length.

Eating in Public

Several kings used to eat in front of other people. One was Louis XIV of France, who took most of his meals in front of a large audience. In Britain in the reign of George II, people could buy tickets to watch the royal family eat their Sunday dinner.

Mammoth Meal

One of the most unusual locations for a dinner party must have been that chosen by Rembrandt Peale in Philadelphia. Thirteen guests sat down to eat and were entertained by a pianist. The whole meal was consumed inside the body of one of the mammoths which Rembrandt and his father had excavated from the Hudson River Valley clay.

High Fiber Diet

They say that fiber is good for you. Jay Gwaltney, aged 19, certainly thought so. In an eating contest in Chicago in 1950, he ate a birch tree that was 11 feet long and had a trunk 5 inches in diameter. It took him 89 hours.

12

Instant Food

In 1982, the *New England Journal of Medicine* reported the craving of an Indian woman for paper. She ate one cigarette packet and a Kleenex box every day. When she was especially hungry she would devour a whole paperback novel.

Wormburgers

The North American Bait Co. once sponsored a 'cookery with worms' competition. The winning recipe was for Earthworm Apple Sauce Surprise Cake!

Frozen Food

Reports of cannibalism are often wildly exaggerated. However, it is recorded that the very first American colonist to be executed had committed this crime. It happened in Jamestown, Virginia, in 1610 after a very hard winter during which there was a terrible food shortage. When the snows cleared it was discovered that one man had managed to survive with the help of his wife. She had died at the height of the cold weather and he had eaten her body.

Mane Course

Horse lovers will be distressed to hear that horse meat used to be, and in some parts of the world still is, enjoyed by many discerning diners. In 1868, a horse meat banquet for 160 was held at the Langham Hotel in London, England. The highlight of the meal was a 264 pound baron of horse which was carried into the dining room on the shoulders of four chefs.

Salt of the Earth

Two hundred years after the execution of King Charles I, Sir Henry Halford, the royal physician, removed a vertebra from the dead king's body. He had it set in gold and he and his family used it as a salt-cellar! Queen Victoria was not amused when she heard about this, and ordered that the bone be returned to the royal coffin. Incidentally, Henry VIII also suffered this indignity as a workman removed a finger bone from his skeleton at the same time and made it into a knife handle.

Body Matters

Until the discovery in the mid-1800s that dirt, germs, and disease all helped to kill people off, washing was not a popular activity. Before this time, the Ancient Romans were just about the only people who enjoyed it. They built large public baths with steam rooms, warm pools, and cold plunges.

After the Roman Empire fell, people quickly lost interest in keeping clean. This caused a lot of problems. Luckily we can only imagine the whiff which must have resulted. The rich could often afford to smother themselves in perfume to disguise the problem. Perhaps the poor smelled so horrible themselves that they couldn't smell other people!

Lack of washing led to infestations of parasites such as fleas and lice, which in turn contributed to the spread of disease, particularly plagues. These were often carried by the fleas living on the rats which flourished in the garbage-filled streets.

Save Water, Bathe with a Friend

The Normans did bathe occasionally, but they were great believers in saving water, probably because it must have been a problem to heat up the large amounts of water needed to fill the big wooden tubs they used.

When bathtime came around, every four months or so, family and guests all bathed together. If there were too many to fit into the tub, they bathed in relays. The last ones out must have been dirtier than when they climbed in!

The Washing Habit

Among the cleanest people in medieval times were monks and nuns. Most monasteries and nunneries had wash-houses and laundries. Monks were given warm water for bathing about four times a year.

Horrible Hair

In the sixteenth and seventeenth centuries, people washed their hair only three or four times a year, on average, using a mixture of wood ash and water as shampoo.

Winter Draws On

In Victorian times, children often had a generous helping of goose grease smeared on their chest to keep out the cold. They were then sewn into their underwear at the beginning of winter, and unsewn at the beginning of spring. Between times, neither child nor garment was washed. In 1840, in Pennsylvania, a law was nearly passed which would have made this practice compulsory.

Hair Grease

The most unhygienic hairdos of all time must have been the high, elaborate hairstyles of the 1770s-1780s. The hair was built up over wire frames sometimes reaching a height of 6 feet, and then decorated. The whole display was greased with a preparation called pomatum (made from apple pressings and hog grease). Flour was patted over this disgusting mess to make the hair white. Naturally enough, vermin were attracted by the smell of the pomatum. Once a week, the head was "opened up" and the vermin "dealt with." If, between cleaning, the itching became unbearable, a sort of miniature back-scratcher with an ivory hand on the end was used to scratch the scalp. Women had to sleep with their heads propped up so as not to squash the frames and only washed their hair about twice a year.

Lice Crispies

Up until the nineteenth century, parasites were an accepted part of life. Almost everyone had fleas and lice. In the seventeenth century, it was considered bad manners to take lice, fleas or other vermin from your body and crack them between your fingernails in company.

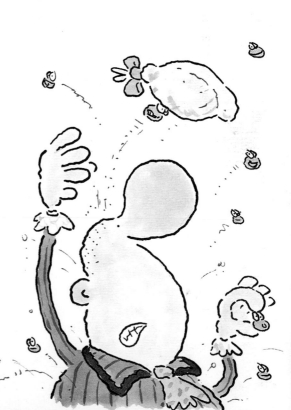

Fatal Face Cream

In Elizabethan and Georgian times, water was considered harmful, so people never cleaned their faces with it. Instead special face wash mixtures were made. These often contained mercury, which is poisonous. After washing, a kind of makeup called ceruse was spread over the face, neck, bosom and arms, which were then glazed with egg white. At one time this makeup was used on the face and neck by men as well. Ceruse contained poisonous white lead. Constant applications of this dangerous mixture led to all kinds of skin diseases. In extreme cases the skin and flesh of the face were eaten away.

Smile Please

Like many people at the time, Queen Elizabeth I of England had horrible teeth which eventually became completely black. Bad teeth were common in Elizabethan times, due to poor diet, lack of hygiene, and people's love of sweetmeats. They did make some effort to clean their teeth, though. The largest chunks of food were dug out with toothpicks. Then they used a toothpowder made from honey, sugar, crushed bones, fruit peel and sometimes soot. To remove stains, they rubbed their teeth with ground pumice stone, alabaster, crushed brick or coral. The mouth was then rinsed with wine or sugary water. No toothbrushes were available (these were not invented until the mid-seventeenth century) so they used a linen tooth cloth to apply the mixture.

Clean Queens

Some queens bathed in very strange liquids to try to preserve their good looks. It is said that Cleopatra used asses milk, while Mary, Queen of Scots, preferred wine.

Good Clean Bess

Elizabeth I, one of the cleanest British monarchs, was determined to set a good example to her subjects. She bathed once a month, whether she needed it or not!

Pungent Palace

During the reign of Louis XIV, the Palace of Versailles was the envy of Europe. It was the most magnificent building, the home of the King of France and about 5,000 courtiers. However, although the ceilings were encrusted with gold and the walls were covered with priceless pictures and tapestries, there were only two toilets. This meant that the less important courtiers were forced to use the marble corridors for personal relief. Richer people could afford their own commode chairs which were carried around the palace until a suitable location was found (usually close to a group of friends so that diverting conversation could take place) where the owner would climb on board.

Whiffy Wife

Public baths opened in Britain in the late seventeenth century, but really only for the wealthy. Samuel Pepys mentions his wife going one day, but this is the only time he mentions his wife bathing in nine years of writing his famous diary.

And While We're on the Subject....

In Charles II's reign, puppy dog urine was recommended for improving the complexion. Samuel Pepys' wife tried it.

17

Ships' Toilets

In Admiral Horatio Nelson's day the toilet arrangements for sailors on warships were very primitive. The seats were placed over the bow. This location was safer and a little more sheltered than elsewhere, but it would hardly encourage loiterers in anything but calm weather, because the spray would have soaked anyone sitting there. However, this sea water must have helped to keep the seats clean. But when the ship was tacking against the wind there was considerable danger that there might be "blow back!" On small ships the sailors had to make do with a bucket on a rope which was dropped over the side to clean it after use.

Ship Fever

Disease was always a danger on board early sailing ships. The importance of eating fresh vegetables was not known and scurvy was a particular problem. Sailors tried to treat themselves by trimming the rotting black flesh from their gums and washing their teeth in urine.

Unsanitary conditions on board and the fact that the wooden eating and drinking utensils were washed in water from the harbor when the ship was in port, helped spread other diseases such as dysentery. Taking on water in the tropics often led to disaster, and resulting infections were spread on board through crowded conditions, poor sanitation, and the numbers of vermin (especially rats). Every ship had its rat population which gnawed and contaminated casks of food. Sailors even ate the rats themselves when food was short.

Towering Toilets

Flushing toilets appeared only recently in human history. Before this people used the great outdoors. If people were indoors they had to do the best they could. Medieval castles had garderobes. These were seats placed over a pipe which carried away the dung through the wall. The dung dropped into the moat or piled up against the castle wall. The smell in summer must have been indescribable. There is no mention at this time of any paper being involved in the process.

Party Potties

At smart dinner parties in the seventeeth century, chamberpots were often provided in dining room sideboards for men, so conversation could continue. People seemed less self-conscious about the procedure than they do today. In the 1660s, Pepys, the famous English diarist, had thought nothing of using the fireplace (servants cleaned up the mess) and wrote that he had caught Lady Sandwich "doing something upon the pot" in the dining room.

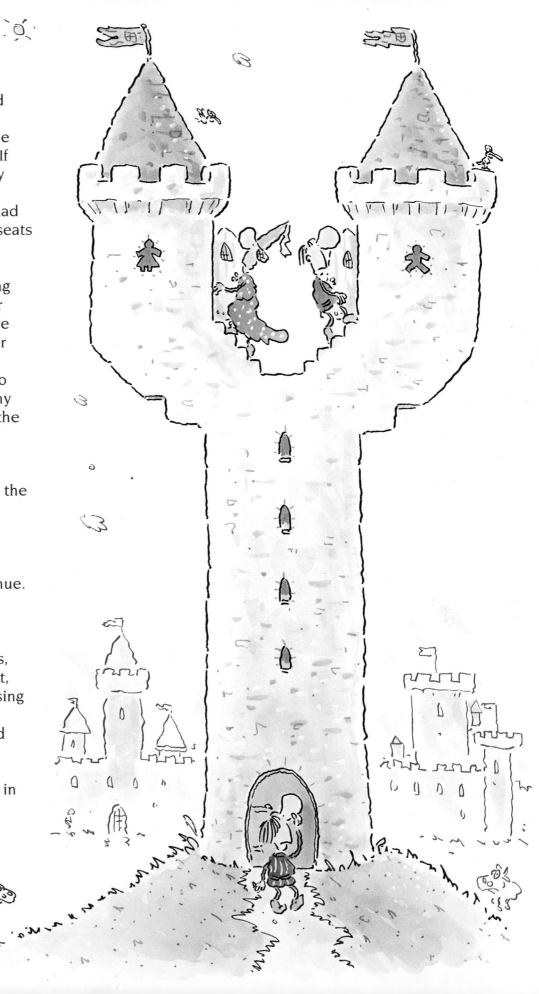

Nasty Jobs

Most people have to work to live. Many have to work very hard indeed or do unpleasant jobs because they are so poor. Perhaps the careers which intrigue us most are those involving dirt or worse! Other people choose, for reasons which ordinary people would find hard to understand, to do jobs which are almost too revolting to describe. Foremost among these are people who willingly inflict pain on others.

Mudlarks

Many people in Victorian England were desperately poor. Some of these, called mudlarks, scratched out a living by searching through river 'mud' at low tide and salvaging anything of value they could find. Since in those days sewage was dumped untreated straight into the river, this must have been unpleasant to say the least. Others approached this work more directly. They haunted the sewers, sifting the muck in the hope of finding valuables which had been "lost" by accident.

Night Workers

During the eighteenth and nineteenth centuries, earth toilets were common. Since the pits had no drainage they would gradually fill up. It was the job of the night soil men to empty them. Moving silently through the night, under cover of darkness, they would arrive at the pit and spoon its contents into large barrels. When the barrels were full, they carried them away – very carefully.

Super Pooper Scoopers

During Victorian times poor children in Britain collected dogs' mess from the streets. They were called "pure finders" and they worked very carefully! The results of their scooping were sold to tanners who used it in the process of turning hides into leather.

Digging for Gold

In Britain, one of the most macabre jobs was body snatching. This grisly trade became popular when medical schools grew desperate for corpses for medical students to dissect. Bodies were hard to come by because most people, even executed criminals, were buried soon after their death. Most body snatchers worked at the dead of night, digging in graveyards unearthing newly buried bodies. The first reported case of body snatching was in 1777 when a corpse was taken from a graveyard in Bloomsbury, London.

Easy Money

Two of the most famous body snatchers, Burke and Hare, developed a cleaner way of finding bodies. They were two Irish emigrants who came to Scotland in about 1820. Hare became the keeper of a lodging house in Edinburgh. One of his lodgers died, owing a large amount of rent. In order to get back some of this money Burke and Hare sold the corpse to a Dr. Knox at Edinburgh medical school for 80 cents. They soon realized that this was an easy way of making money – body snatching without all the digging! When another lodger became sick with fever they suffocated him and sold the body for sixteen dollars. Soon the couple became greedy. They no longer waited for people to get sick. They lured them into the lodging house and then murdered them. At least 15 were killed in this way. This macabre trade was uncovered by a visitor who found a dead body under a bed. Burke and Hare were then arrested. In 1829 Burke was sentenced and hanged for murder. But Hare made a deal with the police and was released.

Just a Wee Job

Collecting and working with human urine has been a human activity for thousands of years. The liquid was mainly used as a cleaning and bleaching agent in the production of cloth. In Roman times slaves washed togas by throwing them into barrels of urine and then treading them rather like winemakers tread grapes. Unfortunately as a result of this many of the slaves developed skin diseases. In Britain during the eighteenth and nineteenth centuries, urine was used by fullers to wash and bleach wool. Mill owners paid the residents of nearby towns and villages a small fee. In return each household stored its urine in a large pot provided by the mill owner. Once a week collectors came round with special carts and took the urine, or "lant" as it was called, away. They were always careful not to spill a drop of the precious liquid!

Fight to the Death

Roman emperors kept the people of Rome happy by providing entertainment. These usually took the form of chariot races or gladiatorial games. Many gladiators were slaves or criminals sent to fight as a punishment. If they survived for five years in the arena they were freed. However, gladiators became very popular. They were as famous as pop stars or film stars are today. As a result many ordinary Roman citizens became gladiators, hoping to win fame and fortune. As the crowds became used to violence and death, the games became increasingly spectacular and bloody. Occasionally entire armies and navies of gladiators fought in the arena, which could be flooded for sea battles. Emperor Trajan staged a combat involving 4,961 pairs of gladiators. Being a gladiator was not a long-term career. The highest number of fights survived by any single gladiator was 88, and we know of one free man, Publius Ostorius, who survived 51 combats.

I'll Serve and You Carve

An unpleasant working partnership developed in England between Judge "Bloody" Jeffreys and executioner Jack Ketch in the late seventeenth century. Jeffreys was appointed to try the rebels who followed the Duke of Monmouth in his attempt to seize the throne. He was completely merciless in his sentencing. When the Duke of Monmouth was about to die Jeffreys insisted on testing the sharpness of the axe and paid Jack Ketch a large bonus for his work. Ketch did not do a very efficient job, however. He chopped at Monmouth's neck three times, but the Duke was still alive. After another two strokes he had not removed the head and was forced to take a large knife to finish the job.

Gutsy Workers

In Ancient Rome, a carefully selected group of priests called haruspices had the job of inspecting the entrails of many different kinds of animals. This was because, like many ancient peoples, the Romans believed that they could read the future from the intestines of sacrificed animals.

Roman Slaves

In many societies, the worst job was to be a slave, because you were just another possession. The Ancient Romans could be particularly cruel owners, often treating their slaves worse than they treated their animals. It is true that very few slaves became rich and powerful, one or two even became emperor's advisers. Most slaves, however, toiled for long hours in more dangerous and uncomfortable conditions than we could imagine. Punishment for slaves could be brutal. Slaves could be flogged or killed at the whim of their owners. The Romans had so many slaves that they were always terrified of slave rebellion. The slightest sign of this danger meant that the owners reacted with swift brutality. One law was particularly cruel. It stated that if a slave killed his or her owner, then every slave in the household should be executed at once.

Which One's a Witch?

In the seventeenth century, Matthew Hopkins became the first "Witch-Finder General" in England. His dreadful job was to travel around the country searching for witches. Hopkins used time honored methods for discovering whether a woman was a witch. Witches were thought to keep an evil spirit called a "familiar" disguised as an animal, usually a bird, a cat, or a toad. Since witches were thought to feed their familiars with their own blood, Hopkins searched for her "devil's mark." Any scar, birthmark or even an insect bite would "prove" that she was a witch. Witches were also "swum." The suspect was tied up, then thrown into a river or pond. If she floated, it proved she was a witch. If she sank, she was innocent, but probably drowned. Other methods included telling the suspect to cry. Anyone who did not shed tears was a witch. Suspects were ordered to say the Lord's Prayer. If they made a mistake, they were immediately found guilty. Yet another test was to weigh the suspect against the large church Bible. The unfortunate woman was declared a witch if the weight of the Bible was more than her own. In this way hundreds of innocent women were condemned and hanged. Among them were 19 women hanged on a single day in Essex, England.

Witch Sniffers

The African Zulus also believed in witches. There were usually many witch-hunters attached to the king's court. Occasionally great "smellings" were held where the witch-hunters sniffed out the "guilty." In this way several hundred suspects were rounded up and executed on the spot. Being a Zulu witch-sniffer was generally a very safe job, since the sniffers were not likely to be accused of being witches themselves. However in 1824 Shaka, King of the Zulus, turned the tables on them. He announced that he had found blood smeared on his house. This was the classic sign of a witch's curse. Shaka called together his 150 finest witch-finders and ordered them to find the culprits immediately. All the Zulus who had been in the area at the time (some 30,000) were gathered. The witch-finders went to work. They moved up and down the ranks of Zulus, smelling and sniffing. As the hours passed more and more people were smelt to be witches. Eventually more than 300 "witches" had been found. They were dragged towards Shaka to meet their death. Shaka then announced that he had smeared the blood himself because he had wanted to test his witch-finders. Obviously they were useless as they had condemned 300 men to death without finding the real culprit. Shaka immediately had the 150 witch-finders clubbed to death.

25

Foul Fashions

There is an argument that, in the days before the importance of equal rights was recognized, what made a woman beautiful was that which reflected the power, position and wealth of her husband. Thus, in Victorian times, pale ladies with a weak constitution were admired because this showed their husbands could afford to have lots of servants to look after them and that they were rich enough not to work. Other cultures, such as the Sioux Indians, apparently admired very fat ladies. This showed that the husband was a great hunter who could feed his wife well. So fashions can differ a great deal according to time and place. One thing we can almost always say is that people often go to enormous lengths and suffer considerable discomfort to follow it.

Hairy Bears

In the eighteenth century, bear grease was a well known hair restorer.

Hairless Ladies

Women of Ancient Rome plucked their eyebrows with tweezers and rubbed the hair off the rest of their body with a pumice stone.

Soft Skin

In prehistoric times, before the invention of weaving, people wore animal skins and pelts. The skins had to be softened by chewing to make them flexible and comfortable enough to wear.

Freckle Face

Freckles have not always been popular. This recipe is taken from an eighteenth century leech book: "To do away with freckles in the face take hare's blood and mix it with swallow's eyes and anoint thee therewith but it must be done anew every year."

Denture Difficulties

In the eighteenth century, some women put little pieces of cork called plumpers into their mouths to replace lost teeth. Sometimes, poor people sold their teeth to rich people for implantation. Teeth were stolen from dead bodies and from dead soldiers on battlefields. These teeth were not always boiled, so when they were implanted into other people's mouths, diseases could be passed on. False teeth did not appear until the late eighteenth century. They were made from bone, ivory or wood, and were tied to the adjoining tooth with gold wire. These teeth often did not fit well. George Washington's false teeth were hinged and had an unnerving tendency to leap out of his mouth when he least expected it. Wax impressions of the mouth and proper fitting porcelain false teeth did not appear until the late nineteenth century.

Stuffed Clothes

During Mary I's reign, fashions worn by the Spanish became popular in England and Europe. Doublets and hose were swelled out with stuffing called "bombast." This was made from rags, flock, horse hair, cotton or bran. If the clothes were torn, the stuffing fell out.

The Earliest Corsets

In many cultures slim waists are thought to be a sign of beauty. Excavations of sites at the Palace of Knossos on Crete show that a very constricted waistline, for both men and women, was popular. Some scientists believe that this could only have been achieved by the wearing of a very tight girdle from childhood.

Trendy Toupées

Wigs have often been popular with both men and women. Louis XIV of France popularized wigs for men and set fashion trends which were copied all over Europe. His wigs were clumsy, full-bottomed affairs made of goat's hair, horse hair, or vegetable fibers. Not only were they very hot to wear, but since people hardly ever washed their hair at this time, they must have been crawling with lice and other parasites.

Ruff! Ruff!

During Tudor times, large starched collars called ruffs became popular. By the end of the sixteenth century, ruffs had grown so big that it is difficult to see how their wearers could have survived at all since it must have been nearly impossible for them to put food into their mouths.

Spots, Moles and Cats

Both men and women in Georgian England had to work very hard to be fashionable. Skin, ruined by mercury-based make-up and overeating, was spotty. Both sexes used cloth patches to cover their blemishes. Some patches were made to look like ordinary moles, others were shaped like stars and moons to be more decorative. One popular spot remover contained finely minced meat. People plucked out their hair to give a fashionably high hair line, and a mixture of vinegar and cat dung was applied to prevent the hair growing low again.

Cutting Collars

During the early 1800s, George "Beau" Brummel was the leader of men's fashion in England. He and other dandies who copied him wore the most fantastic clothes. Beau Brummel was reputed to be so fastidious that he would never set foot on the ground, so as not to spoil his clothes. When he went visiting he always went by carriage or sedan chair carried by servants. He made very high collars popular. Some were so high and so stiff with starch that it was said the wearers cut their ears if they moved their heads too quickly.

Cage Creations

The crinoline, a wooden or metal cage which held the dress away from the body, became fashionable in the second half of the nineteenth century. They were tied to the waist and varied in size from enormous to absolutely ridiculous. Cartoonists had a field day drawing ladies in crinolines stuck in doorways or in other embarrassing situations. It was, for instance, very difficult to sit down modestly in a crinoline which could cause the dress to billow over the head. Crinolines were also heavy to wear, although one designer devised an inflatable rubber crinoline. This was very light and could be inflated to the desired size. Ultimately it proved unsuitable largely due to its unfortunate tendency to puncture at inconvenient or awkward moments!

Free Fall Fashion

The crinoline could be a lifesaver. When a woman tried to commit suicide by leaping off the Clifton Suspension Bridge in Bristol, England, her crinoline acted as a kind of parachute. While she did not exactly float gracefuly down into the river mud, she did at least survive the fall.

Earthshaking Fashions

In about 1925, short skirts became fashionable. Some people were unable to cope with the frequent sight of women's legs. The Archbishop of Naples in Italy announced that the recent earthquake at Amalfi was due to God's anger at a skirt which reached no further than the knee.

Bound to be Trouble

Small feet used to be thought very fashionable in China. Until fairly recently it was common practice for Chinese baby girls to have their feet bound to keep them small. The crippling bandages forced the soft, growing toes to curve under the soles. By adulthood the feet of women treated in this way had completely doubled over.

Getting the Point

Tattoos have always been popular body decorations. The Celts wore them and so did some American Indian tribes. The tattoos were applied by puncturing the skin with a sharp point such as a thorn. Soot or other coloring was then rubbed over the wound. Some Indians had so many tattoos that even when they were completely naked, it looked as if they were wearing a full set of clothes.

Of Course It's Tight!

In the great days of the corset in the eighteenth and nineteenth centuries, women struggled and suffered to make their waists smaller. The corsets, which were stiffened with whalebone or even steel, were very hard to fasten. Mothers were advised to make their daughters lie on the floor, face down, so they could place a foot in the small of the back to obtain the necessary pull on the laces. In later years lightweight winches were used to tighten the laces to their maximum. It is now known that tight corsets restricted the blood supply, damaged the internal organs and even caused cracked ribs. It is no wonder that women at this time seemed to faint so frequently!

Fashionable Drink

In the 1840s, it became fashionable for women to look pale and slightly ill. To help them achieve this effect they stopped using rouge to make their cheeks look pink and started drinking vinegar.

Germ Warfare Suits

In England during the plague of 1665, it was fashionable for doctors to wear robes made of leather which reached the ground. They added gauntlets, broad-brimmed hats and hoods which covered their faces. The hoods had eyepieces made of glass and a bird-like beak which was stuffed with herbs to filter the air. The doctors believed that these clothes would protect them from the plague germs. Whether or not this was true, they must have presented a terrifying sight to their patients.

Unpleasant Priests

One of the most unattractive fashions must have been that worn by Aztec priests. One of their main jobs was to perform human sacrifices, and their fashion made them easily recognizable. They covered their faces and bodies with black paint. They never washed, and their hair was left uncombed and matted with the blood of their victims. Their own bodies were marked with scars where they cut themselves from time to time in order to draw off their own blood to drink.

Brimming Over

In the 1890s, fashionable ladies wore hats with incredibly wide brims. These were very impractical, making it impossible for the wearer to approach close to other people, and very annoying for anyone sitting behind them since they blocked out the view. They could be painful as well. The hats were held in place with long, sharp hat pins through the hair. In strong winds, or on top of an open bus the hat flapped like a sail and could even pull out the wearer's hair. However, the hat pins could be used as weapons by a lady forced to protect herself from any unwelcome advances.

Slow Progress

In about 1910, skirts became narrow at the hem. One fashionable design was called the hobble skirt. It was so tight around the legs that it was almost impossible for the wearer to take a step of more than about 3 inches long.

Inventions

Most of the really horrible inventions were dreamed up many years ago, early in human history. The inventors of devices like the rack and the iron maiden, have either carefully concealed any traces of their involvement, or have simply been forgotten. However, there is a whole catalogue of bizarre inventions. Some of them so mind-numbingly strange and brain-bogglingly useless that one wonders how the inventors ever came to devise them.

Coppery Corpses

In 1891, Dr. Varlot, a surgeon in Paris, developed a method of covering a dead body with a layer of metal in order to preserve it for eternity. The body was made electrically conductive by atomizing nitrate of silver on to it. To free the silver in this solution, the corpse was placed under a glass dome from which the air was evacuated and then exposed to the vapors of white phosphorus dissolved in carbon disulphide. The body was then immersed in a galvanic bath of sulphate of copper, thus causing a 1 millimetre thick layer of metallic copper to be deposited on the skin. The result was a brilliant red durable copper finish.

MON CHÈRE PIERRE
1823 - 1891

32

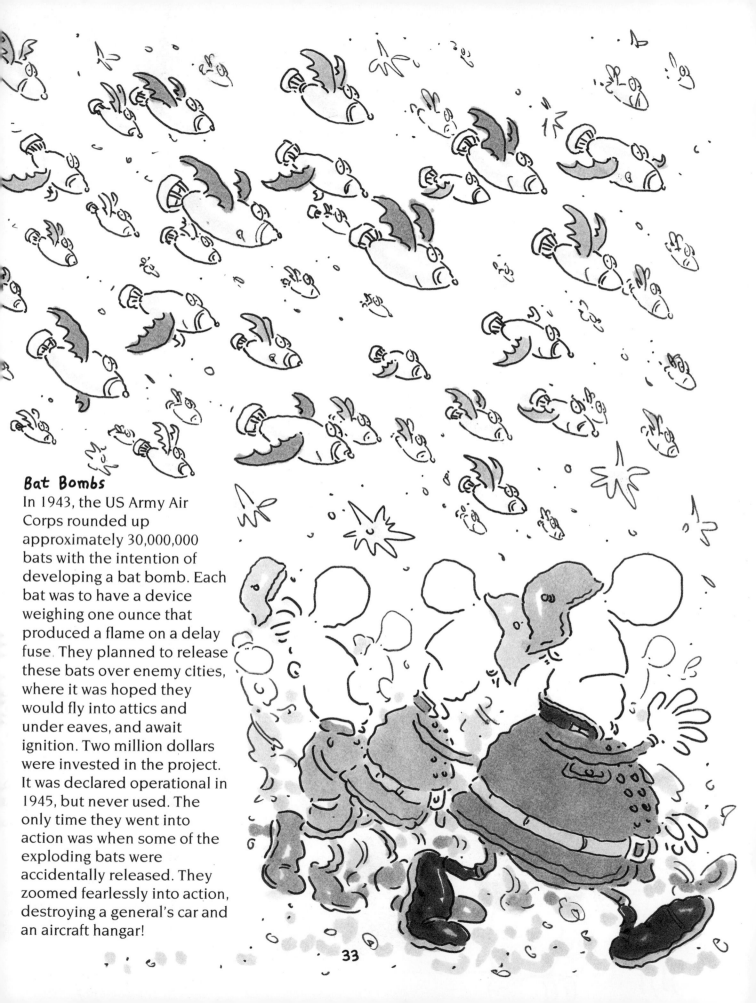

Bat Bombs

In 1943, the US Army Air Corps rounded up approximately 30,000,000 bats with the intention of developing a bat bomb. Each bat was to have a device weighing one ounce that produced a flame on a delay fuse. They planned to release these bats over enemy cities, where it was hoped they would fly into attics and under eaves, and await ignition. Two million dollars were invested in the project. It was declared operational in 1945, but never used. The only time they went into action was when some of the exploding bats were accidentally released. They zoomed fearlessly into action, destroying a general's car and an aircraft hangar!

Wacky Weapons

When World War II broke out, many people wrote to the British War Ministry suggesting ideas for secret weapons. One thought poisoned barbed wire would be useful – one scratch and you would die in agony. However, there was no explanation of what poison would be used, and how the poison would stay on the wire through rain and snow. Nor was it explained how our own troops would handle and erect the lethal wire. Another suggestion was that since migrating birds could enter enemy territory without suspicion and were difficult to search, they could carry plant diseases to ruin the enemy's crops. The idea was dropped when someone pointed out that birds might find it hard to distinguish fields of crops which belonged to the Allies.

Making a Point

Crime of all sorts was common in Victorian London. There was quite a fashion in the criminal classes for mugging. The victim was often strangled. One inventor put forward a simple device to counteract this. It consisted of a metal collar covered in fearsome spikes. The collar was worn under a scarf or cravat. When the strangler placed his hands round the neck, the theory went, the spikes would stab him and prevent a sudden throttling. However, the *Engineer Magazine* which reviewed the invention pointed out that complete protection of the throat would need such a high collar that the wearer was likely to strangle himself!

Canine Car

A vehicle invented by F. Mey of Buffalo, New York in 1870 had a pair of dogs running round inside the front wheels to turn them like a turnspit and move the carriage along.

Keeping your Head

In 1916 Alfred Bacon Pratt of Vermont, invented the helmet gun. The gun was placed into the front of a steel helmet and was fired by pulling a trigger cord with the teeth. Unfortunately history does not record whether the head stayed on after firing!

Home Help

The New Domestic Motor, invented in 1873, was very simple in concept. The power was provided by the housewife. As she rocked backwards and forwards in her rocking chair, ropes and pulleys moved a counterbalanced arm. This provided power to drive a butter churn, a baby's cradle rocker and a multitude of other handy household gadgets.

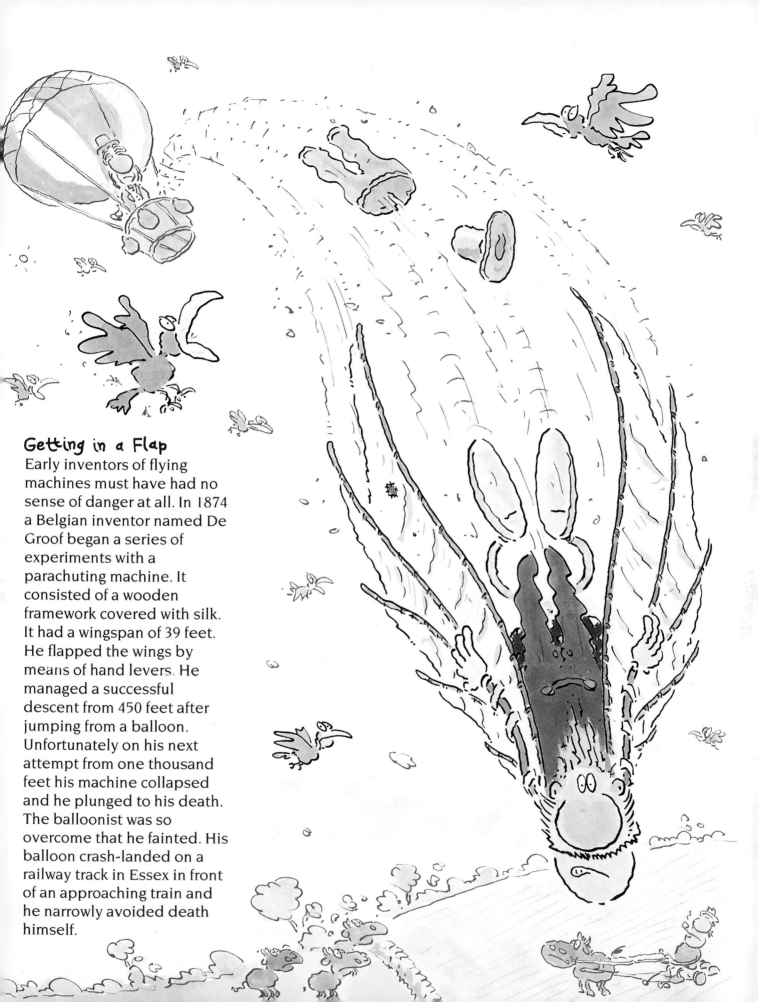

Getting in a Flap

Early inventors of flying machines must have had no sense of danger at all. In 1874 a Belgian inventor named De Groof began a series of experiments with a parachuting machine. It consisted of a wooden framework covered with silk. It had a wingspan of 39 feet. He flapped the wings by means of hand levers. He managed a successful descent from 450 feet after jumping from a balloon. Unfortunately on his next attempt from one thousand feet his machine collapsed and he plunged to his death. The balloonist was so overcome that he fainted. His balloon crash-landed on a railway track in Essex in front of an approaching train and he narrowly avoided death himself.

Horse Powered Stable

In the 1880s an English inventor developed a system whereby a horse could feed and water itself, cleaning its stable at the same time. This complicated machine was worked by a moving floor made from a continuous belt. The horse was supposed to trot along enthusiastically. A clever arrangement of belts and pulleys drove a flour mill, a straw baler and a water pump. A weighted scraper kept the moving belt clean, dropping the manure straight into a cart to be used as fertilizer. Unfortunately for him, his invention was overtaken by the development of the motor car.

Simply Shocking

The electric chair was first used in 1889 in New York. Execution by electrocution was considered a more humane and scientific method of execution than hanging. Poles of a dynamo were connected by a switching device to a metal electrode clamped around the condemned person's head, and to the metal seat of the chair. Sponges or wet cloths were applied at the points of contact to ensure a perfect electrical connection. Extensive experiments were carried out on dogs before the chair was used on humans.

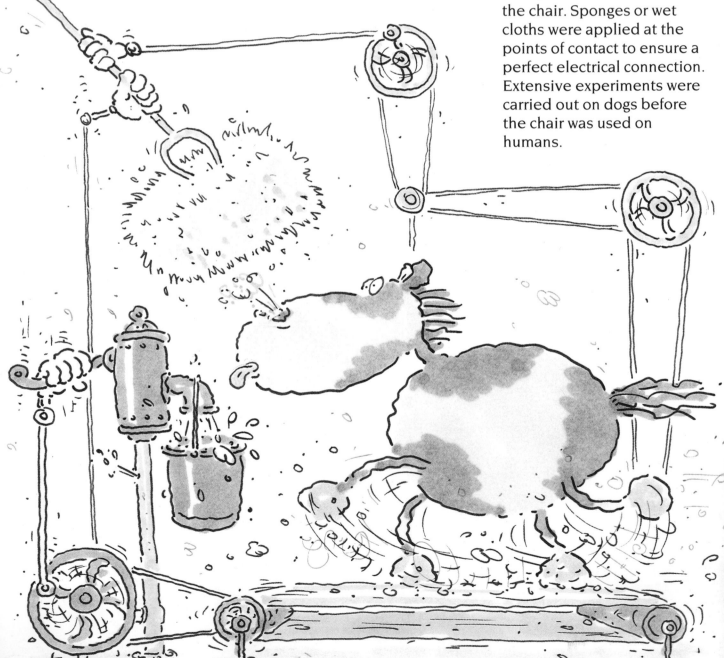

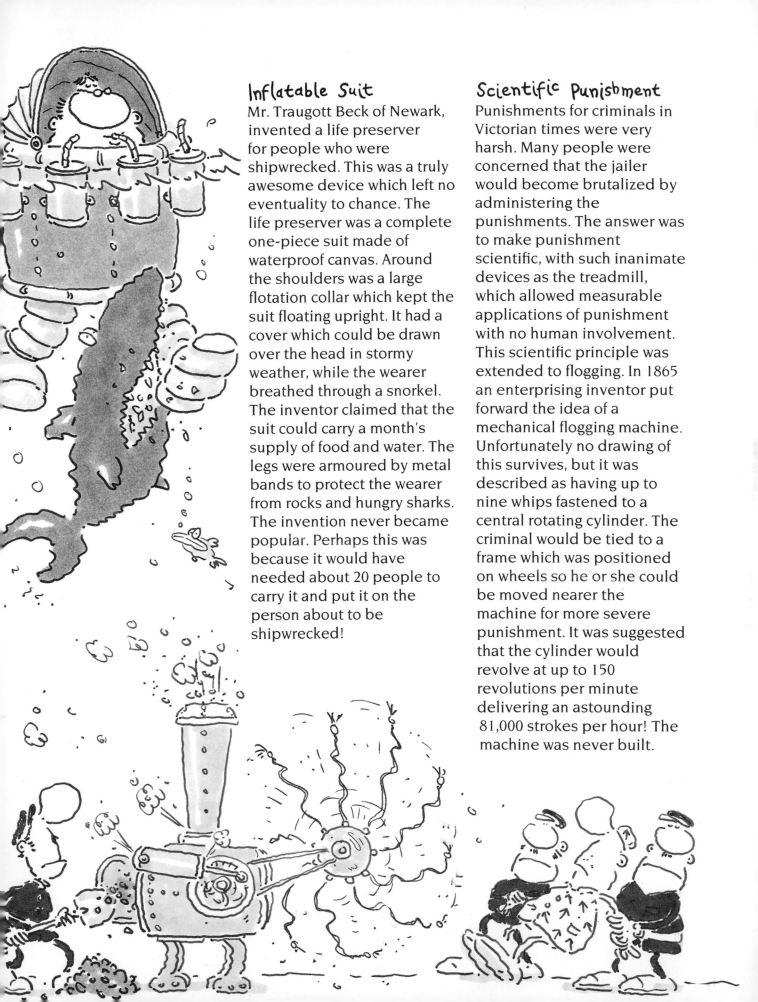

Inflatable Suit

Mr. Traugott Beck of Newark, invented a life preserver for people who were shipwrecked. This was a truly awesome device which left no eventuality to chance. The life preserver was a complete one-piece suit made of waterproof canvas. Around the shoulders was a large flotation collar which kept the suit floating upright. It had a cover which could be drawn over the head in stormy weather, while the wearer breathed through a snorkel. The inventor claimed that the suit could carry a month's supply of food and water. The legs were armoured by metal bands to protect the wearer from rocks and hungry sharks. The invention never became popular. Perhaps this was because it would have needed about 20 people to carry it and put it on the person about to be shipwrecked!

Scientific Punishment

Punishments for criminals in Victorian times were very harsh. Many people were concerned that the jailer would become brutalized by administering the punishments. The answer was to make punishment scientific, with such inanimate devices as the treadmill, which allowed measurable applications of punishment with no human involvement. This scientific principle was extended to flogging. In 1865 an enterprising inventor put forward the idea of a mechanical flogging machine. Unfortunately no drawing of this survives, but it was described as having up to nine whips fastened to a central rotating cylinder. The criminal would be tied to a frame which was positioned on wheels so he or she could be moved nearer the machine for more severe punishment. It was suggested that the cylinder would revolve at up to 150 revolutions per minute delivering an astounding 81,000 strokes per hour! The machine was never built.

Crime and Punishment

Most groups of people have rules or laws to keep their society running smoothly. In the past, when there was no proper police force, punishments were often very brutal, mainly to discourage others from breaking the law.

People who made laws often tried to make the punishment fit the crime. A common punishment for stealing up until the Middle Ages, for instance, was for the criminal to have their hand cut off. Often the criminal was marked in some way, to warn others that they were dishonest. Branding a letter on to the face with a red-hot iron, or disfigurement, such as nose-slitting, were common.

Guilty Pig

Pigs used to roam village streets in France, and the law for people applied to animals as well. In 1547, a sow and her six piglets were accused of beating a child. The sow was hanged, but her family was released on account of their youth and the fact that they had been led astray by the bad example of their mother!

Record Chopping Time
The guillotine was very efficient. In June 1794, 61 victims were executed in 41 minutes. Skilled operators could achieve speeds of more than two EPM (executions per minute).

The Kindest Cut of All
The guillotine was named after a Dr. Guillotin who popularized it as a more humane and less painful way of executing people than the old method of hanging or dismemberment. It was used in France in 1792, and the crowds who watched the execution were disappointed at missing the usual death agonies of the victim. However, as the French Revolution progressed, the crowds grew to enjoy this new method of execution. They cheered as the heads flew off and the guillotine's victims were laughingly described as "sneezing into the basket!"

Variety is the Spice of Death

Methods of execution vary from place to place. Many executions used to take place in public and were purposely made brutal and painful to impress the crowds with the awful fate that awaited wrongdoers. Humans have always been very inventive when it comes to killing each other and methods used have included strangling, stoning, crushing, drowning, poisoning, electrocuting, crucifying, gassing, dismembering, hanging, burning, beheading, burying alive, and feeding to animals.

A Man of Many Parts

For many years in Britain hanging, drawing and quartering was the punishment for treason. The victim was cut down alive from the gallows, the head was cut off, the body quartered and sent to the king, who decided what to do with the bits. In 1305, William Wallace was accused of high treason. After his execution, his head was stuck on London Bridge, his right arm sent to Newcastle, his left arm sent to Berwick, his right leg sent to Perth and his left leg sent to Aberdeen. These various parts were put on display as a warning to others.

Harsh Judgement

In seventeenth century England, Judge Jeffreys was a notorious hanging judge. He condemned hundreds of people during his career. The only slight mercy he ever showed anyone was in the trial of Lady Lisle. At the age of 70, she was tried for treason. Jeffreys was kind enough to allow her to sit during her trial and provided a court official to shout at her, so the old lady (who was stone deaf) could understand what was going on. When she was found guilty Jeffreys put aside all thoughts of mercy, and condemned her to death by burning. However, fortunately for the old woman, her sentence was later reduced to beheading!

A Sailor's Life for Me

Punishments for sailors during the days of sailing ships were very harsh. For minor offences a flogging was common. A special whip, called a cat o'nine tails, made from knotted ropes was used. Sentences of up to 200 lashes with this fiendish instrument were quite common. Victims were often seriously injured. For really serious crimes a sailor would be "flogged round the fleet." He was rowed to every ship in harbor and received a flogging on each one. Not many sailors survived such a punishment.

A Life on the Ocean Wave

Some criminals who are anxious to keep healthy love to take long sea voyages to sunny parts of the world. Here, far from the forces of law and order, they pursue their favorite hobby, piracy.

One of the most famous pirates was Edward Teach, better known as Blackbeard. He began his career in 1716 and sailed the Caribbean in his ship, the *Queen Anne's Revenge*. He was feared by all decent people, partly because of his brutality and partly because of his disgusting appearance. He braided his beard with small pieces of ribbon and curled the strands around his ears. When boarding a ship he wore six pistols in his belt and stuck burning matches under his hat to make himself look fiercer. Someone did love him, however, because he had a wife in London and managed to marry another 14 women during his two-year career.

Blackbeard was eventually killed in a fight against a Royal Navy ship in 1718. The victorious captain cut off Blackbeard's head and hung it on the bowsprit of his ship. The only survivor of Blackbeard's crew, Israel Hands, ended his career as a crippled beggar in London – although he did made a brief guest appearance in Robert Louis Stevenson's book *Treasure Island*.

Your Money or Your Life

Robbing coaches was a cold and risky business. To make sure that they did not return from a night's work empty handed, highwaymen in the 1720s in London were known to attach notices on the doors of rich people's houses. These commanded the occupants, on pain of death, to carry at least thirty-five dollars and a gold watch whenever they went out!

A Taste for Blood

The Hungarian Countess Elizabeth Bathony became convinced that drinking and bathing in the blood of young girls would keep her young and beautiful. At first she and her servants hunted at night for suitable "blood donors" in the villages around her castle. In 1609 she started a school and took in 25 girls at a time, promising to teach them the social graces. She grew careless, however, and she was arrested when the bodies of four girls were found near the castle walls. At her trial evidence was brought which showed she had murdered 600 girls. Her accomplices were burned as witches and the Countess was walled up in a tiny room in her castle. She was fed scraps of food which were pushed through the bars. She died four years later, without a word of remorse.

Babylonian Brutality

Some of the earliest laws were those of Hammurabi, King of Babylon, written in about 2100 BC. They were extremely harsh and demanded punishments to fit the crimes. The penalty for breaking someone's leg, for example, was to have your own leg broken.

Lost Souls

Up until the nineteenth century, suicide was considered a crime so suicides were not buried in churchyards. Suicide cases were often buried at crossroads, with stakes through their hearts. This was because it was a common belief that people buried outside graveyards would return to torment the living unless they were pinned to the spot. However, even if a spirit did escape, it would be confused by the choice of roads.

The Law's an Ass

Some laws seem rather strange to us. You would not expect to be fined for not wearing a woollen cap on Sunday and yet in Elizabethan England a law to help the woollen industry was passed which made the wearing of woollen caps compulsory. At various times people have been punished for taking in relatives who had no jobs, not going to church on Sunday, gossiping, not practicing archery, playing football, playing cards, eating Christmas dinner, and dancing.

Murder Charges

Saxon law set a price on everyone's head. If someone was killed, either murdered or in a "fair" fight, the killer had to pay a fine to the victim's family. The more important the victim, the higher the fine. There were also charges for injury. Cutting off someone's thumb would cost the attacker one

dollar sixty cents. A foot cost four dollars and a big toe eighty cents.

Kill or Cure

People have suffered from disease and pain since they first appeared on Earth about 2½ million years ago. For most of this time doctors had no idea what caused disease or how to cure it. Most medical treatments, apart from a few useful herbal cures, were based on superstition and guesswork. Religious laws which forbade the dissection of human bodies, and complete lack of scientific methods held back the study of medicine for centuries.

Real progress did not really start until the early 1600s when William Harvey discovered that the blood circulated through the body. This started off serious medical research and investigation which continues to this day.

Oh! My Head!

We know from archaeological evidence that the first headache cure was invented in about 8,000 BC. The patient must have been in considerable pain because the cure involved cutting a hole in his head with a chisel! Patients who took this cure never had headaches again – and we have their bodies to prove it!

Tooth Terror

In the Middle Ages, British barber surgeons pulled teeth out with pliers or with a clawed instrument called a pelican. The patient was strapped to a chair, or laid on the floor with his or her head between the dentist's legs. The tooth was wrenched out without any anaesthetic. Some people who had toothaches committed suicide rather than have their teeth pulled.

Quick Quack

One of the fastest dentists on record lived in Victorian times. In order to attract customers, he posed as a Sioux Indian chief, called Sequah, and his cronies dressed as braves. Once the patients arrived he worked at lightning speed. On one occasion he pulled 74 teeth in under an hour. While he worked, a brass band played to drown the screams of his patients.

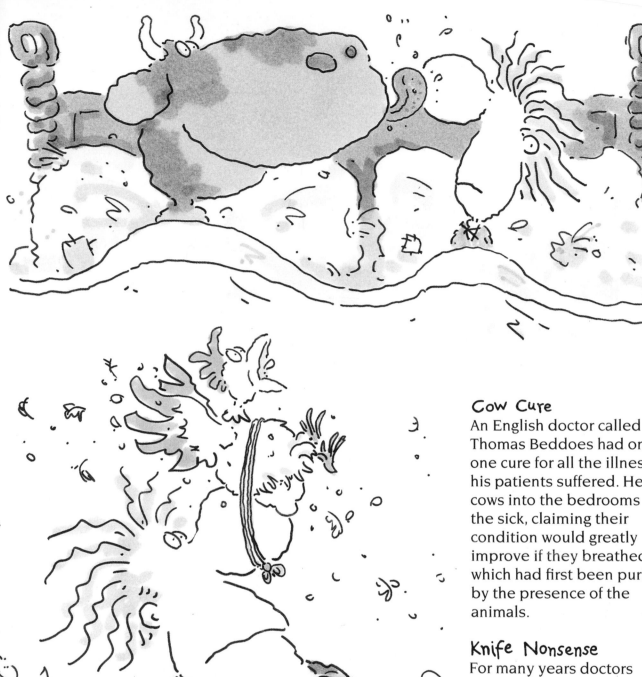

Cow Cure

An English doctor called Thomas Beddoes had only one cure for all the illnesses his patients suffered. He took cows into the bedrooms of the sick, claiming their condition would greatly improve if they breathed air which had first been purified by the presence of the animals.

Knife Nonsense

For many years doctors believed that disease was carried in the blood. While this is quite a sensible idea, they also believed that the way to cure a patient was to let out some of this "bad" blood by cutting one of the patient's veins. Pints of blood might be lost in this way, each "treatment" weakening the patient further. It is surprising that any of those treated in this way recovered at all.

Fowl Cure

Doctors had no real cure for the plague that attacked Europe in the fourteenth century. One doctor, Thomas Vicary, tried a cure based on chickens. How successful it was we don't know. The doctor shaved a chicken's bottom and tied the bird against the swollen parts of the victim. The idea was that the badness would pass into the chicken. Each time a bird became infected it was replaced until either one remained healthy or the patient died.

Royal Death

Death was taken very seriously at the court of Louis XIV at Versailles. When a member of the royal family died, an immediate post mortem was held. The bed chamber was turned into a mortuary and the nobles in waiting, who were often in a state of grief, had to stand and watch while the examination was carried out. While this was going on, half a dozen doctors made notes and pronounced the cause of death.

Draft-Proof Doctor

Monsieur de l'Orme, who was doctor to Louis XIII and XIV, believed that he would live longer if he stayed out of drafts. When at home he sat in a sedan chair covered with blankets and furs so that no air could get in. When he went out, he wore a leather robe and mask, six pairs of stockings and several fur hats. So that cold air could not penetrate his body he always kept a bit of garlic in his mouth, incense in his ears and a stalk of rue sticking out of each nostril. He slept in a brick oven surrounded by hot water bottles. He lived on sheep's tongues and greengage syrup, and never ate vegetables, raw fruit, jam or pastry. He lived until he was 94.

Surprise! Surprise!

Dr. Hugh Thomas, a nineteenth-century medic from Liverpool, England, pioneered a unique form of shock treatment for the sick. He once cured a slipped disc by creeping up behind the patient and delivering a swift kick to her backside. Although his cures were painful, they were often effective. Thomas refused promotion, however, preferring to work with the poor. When he died from overwork in 1891, more than 1,000 people attended his funeral.

Yankee Toothy Dandy

One of the pioneers who led the search for a method to conquer pain was Horace Wells, an American dentist. He believed that nitrous oxide, or laughing gas, could be used as an anaesthetic. He proved this by painlessly pulling out one of his own teeth while breathing the gas. Unfortunately, when Wells tried to demonstrate his method to a group of doctors in Massachusetts, his patient groaned. Wells left the operating room in disgrace.

Hang It All!

The last public hanging in Britain took place in Cornwall in August 1862. The victim was called John Doidge. His death was also the last opportunity for anyone in Britain to take advantage of the legendary cure for a stiff neck – being touched by the hand of a hanged man. Luckily the chance was not missed and two women did arrive at the jail in the early morning asking to be touched by the convict's hand after his death.

Animal Antiseptics

In the Middle Ages in Europe there were two main types of medicine, herbal cures and animal cures. Some of the herbal cures were quite sensible and effective. The animal cures varied in quality. All of them were made from items which were obtained from animals. These could be quite effective, like ointments, made from goose grease, but some were decidedly odd. To cure a headache, for instance, the patient was advised to put newly made goat's cheese mixed with bull's blood on the head. To heal a fracture or broken nose, the patient had either to lay warm bull's dung on the injury, or tie up the fracture with a dog's brain under the bandage. Among the most peculiar cures were those that involved hanging parts of dead animals around the patient's neck until the object rotted and fell off.

Bloodsuckers

During the eighteenth century, many doctors still believed in the medieval idea that illness was caused by bad blood. However, bloodletting was a very dangerous treatment. It not only weakened the patient, it sometimes caused them to bleed to death. Doctors became very keen on using leeches which could suck small amounts of blood from their patients. Leeches became so popular that in one year over 40,000,000 of these slimy little creatures were imported to France from tropical swamps all over the world.

Unhygienic Hospitals

At the end of the nineteenth century, hygiene standards in hospitals were very poor. About half of all hospital patients in England died of infections which they actually caught in the hospital itself.

48

Food for Thought

One of the first investigations into digestion was carried out by the Holy Roman Emperor, Frederick II. He was interested to know what was the best action to take after a meal to aid digestion. He made two men eat large meals. He then ordered one to rest for an hour and one to do exercises. When the hour was passed he had them both killed and cut open. When the contents of their stomachs were examined he saw that the one who had rested had digested his meal better.

Tummy Trouble

Some people, far from eating large amounts, find it hard to eat anything at all. One such person was a 53-year-old patient of Dr. Terrillon in France in 1888. The patient suffered from obstructions in his gullet. Dr. Terrillon cut through his abdominal wall into his stomach and pushed in a rubber tube. The patient was then able to pour gruel and other liquids into a funnel, along the tube and directly into his stomach. The arrangement was not very comfortable, but at least the patient did not starve to death.

Strange Customs

Societies in different parts of the world have developed in different ways. The climate, the fertility of the crops, invasions, religion and history all affect the way a society is run, and the customs it follows. Many foreign customs seem strange to us, but make perfect sense to the people who observe them. We are in no position to criticize a custom before we understand the background to it. In many cases history has overtaken the custom which has, as a result, died out – to the relief of all concerned.

Palace Politeness

Louis XIV was keen to keep an eye on the French nobles who had in the past proved rebellious. In order to do this he built the palace of Versailles and brought them there. He diverted their energies by creating a complicated system of etiquette. They were so busy trying to be polite that they had no time to plot against him. The rules were very complicated. No one could turn their back on a member of the royal family, nor on a royal portrait. Knocking at a door was considered very rude, so people scratched with a fingernail. There were several great ceremonies each day which centered around Louis XIV. Among these were the King's "lever" when he rose from his bed, and his "coucher" when he returned to it at night. Small groups of nobles were allowed to be present at each ceremony and to help. Since this was an excellent opportunity to whisper requests to the king, the nobles squabbled jealously to become holder of the royal left sock or remover of the royal underpants!

Ouch!

There are many different fighting sports which are enjoyed all over the world by people who like that kind of thing. One of the simplest was the noble art of shin kicking which was practiced in England until the seventeenth century. Single contestants fought each other, wearing iron-tipped boots. The rules were quite straightforward – each kicked at the shins of the other until one was unable to stand or else gave up in agony. Even players who were quite expert in this sport limped heavily.

Foot Funeral

Burial customs can sometimes be a little strange. None could be stranger than that held by General Santa Anna, winner of the battle of the Alamo. Santa Anna was wounded in a battle and his leg was amputated. Four years later, having become the effective ruler of Mexico, he paraded his leg through the streets of Mexico City. The leg was then given a full funeral ceremony and buried.

Sounds Fishy

When Iroquois women were planting corn, they left dead fish under each seed to fertilize it.

Chilly Childhood

The Ancient Spartans were famous for their fighting skills. They achieved this reputation the hard way. All male babies were inspected and any which looked weak were left on a mountain to die of exposure. Those considered tough enough began their training at the age of seven. They were not allowed to wear any clothes until they were twelve!

Court Battle

An English medieval custom was for an accused person to settle a dispute by fighting. This was called trial by battle. When a proper legal system was introduced, this custom fell by the wayside and remained forgotten for 200 years. But by an oversight no one thought to repeal the laws which allowed it. In 1817 a man called Thornton was brought to trial for the murder of a woman called Mary Ashford. Thornton claimed the right to prove his innocence in a trial by battle with the dead woman's brother. The courts had no choice but to uphold his right. However, the brother refused the challenge and Thornton walked away a free man. The law was changed a year later.

Taking a Serious View

Drunkenness was considered a very serious crime by the Aztecs and was punished by death.

Ruling from Beyond the Grave

The Incas of Peru thought of their kings as gods. The mummified bodies of past kings were brought out each day and paraded in the center of Cuzco, their capital city. The corpses were honored with prayers and sacrifices of white llamas.

Your Money or Your Life

In seventeenth century Britain it was the custom to display the bodies of highwaymen as a deterrent to others. After the highwayman had been hanged, his body was put into a metal frame of chains and bands. This was then suspended from a post or tree at a suitable location, such as a cross-roads. The smell of the decaying body and the grisly sound of rattling chains, served as a warning to others.

went alone with him on a six-hour journey from Versailles to Fontainebleau. She did not visit the lavatory before she left and soon realized she should have done so! She had to wait the whole six hours, despite nearly fainting several times, before she could relieve herself.

Funeral Fun

Gladiatorial combats were very popular in Ancient Rome. Originally they were religious performances put on as part of Etruscan funeral ceremonies. The idea was that the dead person would be revitalized by periodic offerings of blood. The more vigorous the fight, the better quality the blood would be. Milk and wine were poured on the spot where the fighter fell. The Romans adopted the custom and began to put on bigger and better shows. Large gladiatorial contests became a method by which the emperor could keep the favor of the critical and rebellious citizens of Rome. Emperors were judged by the splendor of the performances they staged. One of the most spectacular must have been that put on by Emperor Trajan. His gladiatorial games lasted over four months and involved nearly 10,000 gladiators.

Toilet Training

When traveling from one of his houses to another, Louis XIV liked to be accompanied by women. These journeys were pure torture for his companions. The windows of the carriage were always left open, even in the coldest weather, because he could not bear stuffiness. The ladies were expected to be cheerful, eat a great deal, and have no physical needs which might force them to leave the coach. One duchesse, daughter of his chief minister,

Wailing Widows

In the palace of Versailles in the reign of Louis XIV it was the fashion to grieve out loud. Women who had lost a husband or son at war were expected to appear in the public rooms and make as much noise as possible.

Ancient Animal Lovers

Ancient Romans loved animals, especially when they could watch them fight to the death! Huge amphitheaters were built to stage these spectacles. In Pompeii as in Rome, gladiators were more popular than actors. In 80 BC a huge amphitheater was built in Pompeii, designed to hold 20,000 spectators. Here immense massacres of wild beasts and men took place. Venationes, or sham hunts of wild beasts, were very popular. Unusual types of animals were matched against each other – a crocodile against a leopard, for instance. Before the fight, the animals were maddened by spear thrusts through grilles separating them from the front row of the audience.

These hunts ended in the animals being killed, either by each other or by gladiators. One single event in the reign of Emperor Marcus Aurelius consisted of

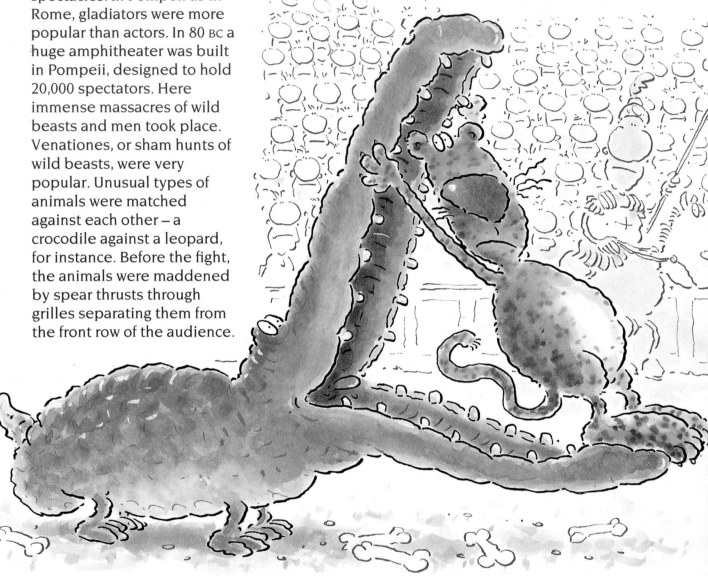

100 lions being shot by archers in the space of a few minutes. So many wild animals were killed that there was a shortage of beasts. Teams of hunters scoured Africa for fresh animals.

Wicker Work

The druids of Celtic Europe practiced an obscure religion about which little is known. However, they were believed to conduct ceremonies in forest glades which involved human sacrifice. One method they used was to build a huge human effigy of wicker. This was, in reality, a cage. Victims were put into the wicker man which was then set on fire. The Romans were revolted by the Druids and their practices, which seems odd considering the wholesale slaughters they organized in the arena, and systematically wiped out the Druids.

Well, Well!

The Mayans of Central America believed that the gods could communicate with them if the circumstances were right. In one Mayan city there were two deep wells. One was for drinking, the other was only used in times of crisis. Then, at dawn, a young woman was thrown into the water 60 feet below. At midday she was hauled out. If she had survived she was asked what the gods had told her, and the Mayans then acted on what she said.

A Barrel of Fun

In Britain on November 5 it is customary to burn an effigy of Guy Fawkes on a bonfire to celebrate the failure of a plot to blow up the Houses of Parliament. However, the people of Ottery St Mary in Devon go one step further than this. They coat nine barrels, the largest being a huge sixty-five gallon hogshead, with tar and set fire to them. The men of the town then carry these blazing barrels through the streets on their shoulders, only putting them down when the barrels disintegrate. No protective clothing is allowed. The odd thing is that the strange ceremony is nothing to do with Guy Fawkes, but is intended to celebrate the landing of the Protestant king, William III in 1688.

Royal Rascals

We might think that kings and queens should set us all a good example by behaving perfectly at all times. However, this is not the case! Royals are capable of bad behavior just like the rest of us. In fact, in many cases their actions are worse because they also have, or had, the power of life and death over their subjects. So their bad behavior can have very unpleasant and far-reaching consequences.

Eadwig the Enthusiastic

The Saxon King Eadwig (who ruled from 955–959) was so in love with his girlfriend that he could not keep away from her. He scandalized his courtiers when he walked out of an important feast which was being held to celebrate his consecration as king, in order to visit her. His courtiers had to rescue the crown from where it had been thrown, separate the couple and then drag him back.

No Smoking!

Britain's James I (king from 1603 to 1625) was in many ways an unattractive man and a dull king. However, in one respect he was far ahead of his time in that he was one of the first anti-smoking campaigners. He described smoking in a pamphlet he wrote as, "A custom loathsome to the eye, hateful to the nose, harmful to the brain, and dangerous to the lungs."

The House where Norman Lives

Edward I of England (who ruled from 1272 to 1307) was famous for his luck. Once he was playing a game of chess with his knights and for no apparent reason suddenly got up and walked away. Seconds later a massive stone, which would have crushed him completely, fell from the roof on to the very spot where he had been sitting.

A Rough Knight

Edward I's son, the Prince of Wales, was knighted in 1306. At the ceremony another 300 men were knighted. The crush round the altar was so dense that two knights died, several fainted and many others had to be taken away for medical attention.

Phantom Pregnancy

James II was anxious to have an heir. However, the circumstances surrounding the unexpected birth of his son were mysterious. Many claimed that his wife Mary was too old to have a child and some said that she had faked her pregnancy. The illusion of birth was created when a substitute child was smuggled into her bed in a warming pan.

An Unfortunate Christening

Ethelred the Unready (king from 979 to 1016) is one of the few English kings about whom hardly anyone has anything good to say. Even the omens at this christening were bad. Those present were horrified when the Prince urinated into the font during the ceremony.

Pleased to Meet You!

George III was an honest, straightforward man who enjoyed nothing more than a simple meal and a session of country dancing. Unfortunately he suffered three periods of madness during his reign. These may have been caused by the strain of arguments with his eldest son and his ministers, or by a disease, or by lead poisoning caused by the containers which held his favorite sauerkraut and lemonade. It was during one of these bouts of madness when he is said to have dismounted from his coach in Windsor Great Park and shaken hands with an oak tree under the impression that it was Frederick the Great.

Brandy Nan

Queen Anne (who reigned from 1702 to 1714) was shy, stout, near-sighted and suffered from gout. She was described as "one of the smallest people ever set in a great place." One of her favorite activities was card-playing and she was a tremendous gambler. She suffered from ill health and in her pain turned to laudanum and brandy. Suffering from gout she became the only British monarch who had to be carried to her coronation. As she lay on her deathbed doctors tried every desperate remedy they knew. These included bleeding, red hot irons to blister her skin, mixtures to make her vomit, covering her feet in garlic and, the final indignity, shaving her head completely bare.

Eccentric Wife

Prince George's wife was Caroline of Brunswick, who had some unfortunate habits. She boasted that she spent very little time washing, she could not dress herself well and sometimes put her clothes on back to front. Once she had a rotten tooth pulled and sent it to George as a souvenir.

Hey Big Spender!

Prince George, who later became George IV, was not only a heavy drinker, and a gambler, but he was also a compulsive spender. Every week he bought huge quantities of creams, perfumes, powders and oils to keep himself looking attractive. This was rather hard work because he was very stout and had an unpleasant, red complexion. He brought everything in large quantities – toothbrushes three dozen at a time and on one day, 32 walking sticks.

Exploding Coffin

At the time of his death, George IV was enormously fat. Only two months before his death he was eating huge meals. One consisted of a massive quantity of roast beef, two glasses of hot ale, toast, three glasses of claret, some strawberries and a glass of brandy. He died soon after! As he was lying in state in a lead coffin, his decomposing body began to swell. The lead was seen to bulge dangerously. To stop the coffin from exploding, the lead was punctured to let out the gas, and then recovered.

Royal Flush

Britain's Queen Victoria was rather too proper to misbehave herself, but her rather innocent outlook on life sometimes caused amusing or embarrassing incidents. One of these occurred when she was visiting Cambridge in 1843. At that time all the sewage from the town went straight into the river. As Victoria peered into the water she asked what all the pieces of paper were that she could see floating down the river. There was a short pause and then her host, the Master of Trinity, replied with great presence of mind that they were notices that bathing in the river was forbidden. Victoria was completely satisfied with this answer.

Tally-Ho!

Queen Victoria's son, Prince Edward (later Edward VII), had to wait many years to come to the throne. He enjoyed life immensely, dined well, enjoyed going to the races, and had a great many girlfriends. He was a popular figure, nicknamed 'Tum-Tum,' whose pranks and escapades amused the public. On one occasion he decided to go hunting in London. A deer was brought in for the day. The hunt began in Harrow and ended in the goods yard of Paddington Station. The Prince also took a hunting party up the Nile. They traveled in six steamers which carried 3,000 bottles of champagne, 4,000 bottles of claret, four French chefs and a laundry.

Horse-Loving Emperor

The Roman Emperor Caligula (AD 12–41) was almost certainly mad. His behavior, even for a Roman emperor, was abominable. He made his horse, Incitatus, a senator. It wore purple robes, lived in a marble stable, and had its own slaves. Caligula's catalogue of crimes is far too long to list here. It is enough to say that he enjoyed watching prisoners being tortured while he ate and always made parents attend the execution of their children. He poisoned dozens of people, and may have killed the previous emperor, Tiberius. He never kissed his wife without saying, "And this beautiful throat will be cut whenever I please." Caligula was eventually assassinated.

Nature Lover

George V was a great animal lover. Once, when he came across a dead bird in the garden at Windsor, tears came to his eyes. On the other hand he also enjoyed shooting. On one shoot at Windsor, the King and six other guns killed over 10,000 birds. Like most people at that time, George found nothing contradictory in his two very different views of wildlife.

Burning Ambition

The Roman Emperor Nero (AD 37–68) was another unpleasant character. When his pregnant wife complained that she was tired after a day at the races he kicked her to death. He murdered almost every member of his own family. He tried to poison his mother three times; when that failed he rigged up a machine in her bedroom to crush her; she was warned so he had a collapsible boat built; the ship sank but she swam ashore so finally he had her killed in a way that it looked like suicide. He had his stepson drowned simply because the boy had played at being a general and emperor. He ordered the city of Rome, which he wanted to rename Neropolis, burned to the ground. He then opened a fire relief fund to which everyone had to contribute. Finally, deserted by his supporters and bodyguards, and threatened by rebellion, Nero commited suicide.

Temper, Temper!

Tsar Ivan IV of Russia (1530–1584) was a strong ruler who greatly increased the prestige and power of Russia. However, the death of his wife seemed to effect his mind. He became convinced that he was surrounded by people plotting against him. His chief suspect was the Bishop of Moscow whom he had horribly strangled. Soon after this, in a fit of insane rage, he killed his own son. He turned his anger against the city of Novgorod, which he attacked and burned to the ground, massacring all the inhabitants. In his later years he began carrying a long staff with a sharp iron point. When in a temper he used it to stab whoever was standing nearest to him. It's no wonder that he became known as Ivan the Terrible.

Admiring the View

In his later years the Roman Emperor Tiberius (42 BC–AD 37) became exceedingly cruel. He hated Rome and went to live on the island of Capri. Here, in great luxury, he occupied his days with activities most of which are too horrible (or too complicated) to describe even in this book! He enjoyed sitting in the garden seat at the top of a cliff admiring the view. Now and then, as an extra diversion, he liked to watch prisoners being tortured in front of him. When he finally tired of the spectacle he asked for them to be removed from his presence. The quickest way out of the garden was over the cliff. Guards were stationed below to make sure the victims were dead on arrival.

The Personal Touch

Peter the Great, Tsar of Russia, was determined to modernize and strengthen his country. Having crushed a rebellion, he ordered that 14 torture chambers be built. Huge numbers of captured rebels were "put to the question with lash and fire" – over 1,700 in one month alone – and then executed. Peter certainly attended many of these torture sessions and probably personally beheaded several of the rebels.

Arguments, Quarrels and Worse

Throughout history human beings have argued, quarrelled, fought and killed each other. We have, throughout our existence, used our "superior" intelligence to invent new and more efficient ways of wiping each other out. Unlike other animals, humans are able to join together into large groups to attack members of their own species. It seems strange that we, with our ability to communicate, should have spent so much time and energy doing exactly the opposite.

First Fight

Humans have probably fought each other from the first moment they evolved. However, the earliest known weapon is a spear found in Essex, England in 1911. It was a mere 200,000 years old.

What's This 'ere?

One of the strangest causes for a war occurred in 1739. England and Spain were not on good terms at the time. An English sailing ship had been stopped by Spanish coastguards in the Caribbean. The Spanish demanded the English pay heavy taxes and tortured them when they refused. The captain, Robert Jenkins, had his ear cut off by one of the Spanish coastguards who told him to show it to his king. Jenkins picked up his ear and put it in a box. Eventually he took his ear to Westminster and showed it to the members of Parliament. Naturally they were all disgusted by the grisly sight. This was hardly surprising since the ear had actually been cut off eight years earlier in 1731! England promptly declared war on Spain. The war became known as the "War of Jenkins' Ear."

The Blind Leading the Blind

Tsar Basil of Byzantium took a terrible revenge on a Bulgarian army he defeated in 1014. Having surrounded and defeated the Bulgarians, Basil ordered that the 15,000 survivors should be blinded. One man in every hundred had only one eye put out, so they could lead the blind army home. When the pathetic remnants of his forces arrived, Tsar Samuel of Bulgaria is reputed to have been so shocked that he died of a stroke.

Insultin' Sultan

Luckily not all wars are so long or costly. The shortest war on record was fought between Britain and Zanzibar in 1896. Sultan Khaled had seized the throne and refused to give it up until a British fleet, led by Sir Harry Rawson, bombarded the palace. The war actually lasted 38 minutes. Sultan Khaled was replaced by Sultan Hamid ibn Mohammed, who immediately awarded Sir Harry a large medal.

Just the Biggest

The bloodiest war in history was World War II. During the six years of fighting about 56 million people died, roughly the same number who live in Great Britain today. This war was also the most expensive, costing more than all the other wars ever fought put together.

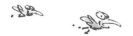

Aerial Aggravation

At various times in history, duelling has been a popular method for settling arguments between individuals. Of course, the only thing a duel actually proves is who is the best shot or the finest sword fighter. One of the strangest duels ever fought was in 1878 in Guyana. It appears that Senor Molica, a Portuguese gentleman, sent a challenge to a Dutchman who, therefore, by the rules of duelling had the choice of weapons and manner of meeting. He chose pistols and balloons! Each climbed into his balloon and floated up to a given height. They then blazed away at each other with pistols. Senor Molica was slightly wounded, but the Dutchman was unfortunately killed.

Scarf Stranglers

The word 'thug' comes from a Hindi word describing the followers of the cult of thuggee. The thugs were required by their religion to murder and then rob their victims in honor of Kali, the Hindu goddess of destruction. They were not allowed to spill blood so their method of killing was to strangle their victims with a silk scarf weighted at one end with a coin. It is estimated that over 2,000,000 Indians were strangled by thugs between the years 1550 and 1853.

Easter Monday Massacre

Some arguments quickly get out of control. On Easter Monday in 1282 a French soldier insulted a Sicilian woman outside a church in Palermo. The woman's husband stabbed him. Other Sicilians then attacked the rest of the French soldiers who were watching. The news spread like wildfire throughout the island and the Sicilians fell on the French, massacring thousands of men, women and children, including soldiers, monks and all the sailors of the French fleet in Messina harbor.

Relaxing

Some of the bitterest quarrels have been over religion. In the Middle Ages, the Catholic church set up the Inquisition to discover unbelievers or heretics. After being arrested, the suspects were tortured. If they refused to retract their heretical views, they were "relaxed." This meant that they were burned at the stake. Although the number of deaths at the hands of the Inquisition has been greatly exaggerated over the years, it is likely that several thousand heretics were "relaxed" in this way.

A Golden Moment

All wars are terrible, but civil wars seem even worse. The bloodiest civil war in history was fought in China. The peasant rebels were led by Hong Xiuquan, who believed he was the younger brother of Jesus Christ. Hong called the war T'ai P'ing, which means "Great Peace." During the war, which lasted from 1851–1864, roughly 30 million people died. Faced with final defeat Hong, who was clearly mad, killed himself by eating gold leaf – surely one of the most exotic and expensive methods of committing suicide ever devised!

Author of his Own Death

Many quarrels have been the result of fits of bad temper. One such occurred in Basra in 737 when the great Arabic writer Ibn al-Mukaffa was tortured nearly to death on the orders of Caliph al-Mansur. Following this, his limbs were cut off and the rest of his body thrown alive into a hot oven. This horrible fate was earned because the Caliph had asked al-Mukaffa to write a pardon for a rebellious noble. Ibn al-Mukaffa was over-enthusiastic with his task and wrote in the document so many oaths for the Caliph to swear that the ruler became enraged and ordered the writer's death.

Zulu Tyrant

Shaka was one of the greatest Zulu chiefs. However, as he conquered neighboring tribes and his empire grew, he became increasingly cruel. In 1827, his mother died. Shaka was very upset, partly because many of his subjects, whose eyes were dry, were not sad enough. As a little gesture to show his disapproval at their lack of grief he had over 7,000 of them put to death. When two of his brothers killed him in 1828 there was no outcry.

A Victory against Great Odds

One of the most successful generals must be Richard, the English Earl of Pembroke who was known as Strongbow. He landed in Ireland in 1169 with just 10 knights and 70 archers and defeated an Irish army of 3,000 soldiers!

Parting Gesture

In 1327 Mohammed bin Tughluq argued with the citizens of Delhi who had threatened revolt against him. He ordered the inhabitants to leave their homes and move to a new capital city over 500 miles away. Only two citizens were unable to obey the order. One was blind and the other a cripple. However, the Emperor was merciless and ordered these two killed in his favorite manner. One was fired from a cannon and the other had his limbs torn off.

Picking a Quarrel

The Imam Idris and the Caliph Harun al-Rashid of Baghdad had a long-standing quarrel. This stemmed from the fact that Idris, a descendent of the prophet Mohammed, had taken part in a failed revolt against the Caliph in 786. The Imam took refuge in Morocco but the Caliph took his revenge five years later. He murdered the Imam at long range by means of a poisoned toothpick he sent as a present.

Quarrels over Cards

Eighteenth-century Bath was a fashionable spa town in south-west England where the wealthy relaxed. To amuse themselves in the evening they played cards and gambled heavily. This led to many quarrels and several duels. There are stories of cheats being thrown out of windows by their furious victims. On one occasion a gentleman suspected he had been cheated by an opponent who was palming cards. He seized a large, sharp two-pronged fork and stabbed downwards, pinning the trickster's hand to the table, saying in a low voice, "Sir, if you have not a card hidden beneath that hand I shall gladly apologize." No apology was necessary.

Odds and Ends

There is some history which does not fit comfortably into any particular category. Some incidents are really horrible, but others are just amusing. All are too interesting to ignore.

High Temperature

Louis XIV's daughter-in-law went through a considerable ordeal giving birth to her first child. Even though France was in the grip of a heat wave, her doctor, Clement, had a sheep killed in her room and then wrapped her in the skin. This cured her very quickly. She then longed for sleep, but Clement would not allow it. She was forcibly kept awake for several hours. After that her room was sealed up and she had to stay in bed there, in the heat wave, without even the light of a candle, for another nine days.

Being Neighborly

The cure for rabies, as decreed by law in eighteenth-century Ireland, was to smother the patient between two feather beds and then to get a "sufficient number of the neighbors lying on it" until the patient was out of danger.

Manhattan Mobs

Nineteenth-century New York City was a dangerous place, terrorized by criminal gangs with the most extraordinary names and habits. The Dead Rabbits (Irish men who fought under a rabbit impaled on a spike), the Plug Uglies, the Molasses Gang (who specialized in ramming a hatful of molasses over their victim's head), the Daybreak Boys (killers aged 10 or under), the Swamp Angels (who used the sewer system for raids and escapes), and the Charltons (who were led by Sadie the Great).

Deadly Fleas

The Black Death which reached Europe in 1347 killed 30,000,000 people, about a quarter of the population. It had already killed 45,000,000 people in Asia. The deaths were caused by bubonic plague carried by fleas which lived on rats. An effective vaccine was not developed until 1893. The last major outbreak was in 1910 in Siberia when 60,000 people died.

Equine Eccentricity

After the Battle of Waterloo, the then Duke of York had a corridor of his home, Oaklands in Surrey, England, lined with the teeth of horses killed in the battle.

Shaving Superstition

Tsar Peter the Great was determined to Westernize Russia. One of his laws was that no one should wear a beard. He helped to enforce this law himself by pulling out by the roots any beard he saw. However, many superstitious people believed that they would not be allowed into heaven without them. They shaved their beards off to avoid the Tsar's anger, but kept them in their pockets to produce on Judgement Day.

Pet Food

Wild beasts were kept in the Tower of London for centuries. Henry I kept a polar bear there. Hundreds of years ago, visitors to the menagerie could either pay an admission fee of a few cents, or provide a cat or a dog to be fed to the lions.

Cheap Labor

In Catherine the Great's Russia a pedigree dog was worth more than a serf.

Hot Drinks

Traveling long distances through hostile terrain can be very difficult. In desert areas lack of water poses a special problem. In the past people had fewer qualms than we have when it came to survival. A thirsty Mongol warrior would think nothing of cutting open one of his horse's veins and drinking the blood. He then sealed the wound until it was time for the next emergency drink. Even further back in the past, the Qedar tribe of the middle east survived in the desert by cutting open a camel. They then drank its blood and cut out the camel's bladder which could supply several quarts of life-giving fluid. The Apache Indians used their horses in the same way. Of course these measures were only taken in extreme emergencies. If the traveller killed his or her mount, the rest of the journey had to be made on foot.

Survival of the Fittest

One of the best examples of the principle of survival of the fittest occurred in 1816, when the French frigate Medusa sank in the Atlantic. One hundred and forty-seven crew members survived the wreck. Their raft was too small for this number and when they were rescued 12 days later, only 15 remained. The rest had either been thrown overboard or else eaten by the strongest.

A Grave Ceremony

The city of Ur in Ancient Sumeria is famous for its royal tombs. Not only were the kings and queens buried with their treasure and favorite possessions, but they were accompanied by their servants as well. One of these royal graves holds the bodies of 74 royal attendants. It seems likely that, while still alive, they accompanied the body into the tomb which was then sealed. The servants in the grave then all took poison. Several chariots were also put in the grave complete with the bulls which pulled them. The animals must have been poisoned as well. Similar tombs from the Shang dynasty in China have been found. However, the servants in these graves were beheaded before being buried.

73

Ice Queen

Queen Christina of Sweden gave up the throne in 1654 because she became bored. She never married and spent most of her time dressed as a man, traveling round Europe. While in France she suspected that her equerry (officer in charge of horses) was disloyal. Pretending she suspected another of her servants she asked what the punishment should be. Her equerry advised death. Christina coolly called in her guards, reminded her equerry of what he had said, and then ignoring all pleas for mercy ordered him to be stabbed to death in front of her.

Flat Fashion

So they would have a fashionably flat skull, children of Chinook Indians were strapped between boards from their head to their toes until they were about one year old.

The Green Light

The world's first traffic lights were erected in 1868 near the Houses of Parliament in London. They consisted of revolving green and red gas lights. They blew up soon after they were installed, badly injuring the policeman operating them.

Fiery Preacher

The Archbishop of Mainz, Germany had a cure for the great famine of 914. He gathered a large number of poor peasants into a barn on the pretext of feeding them, and then set fire to the building. Not only did this reduce the number of mouths there were to feed, but by sending all those poor people to heaven he believed that God would be persuaded to end the famine. The story has a happy ending, though. Years later he was eaten alive by hordes of mice!

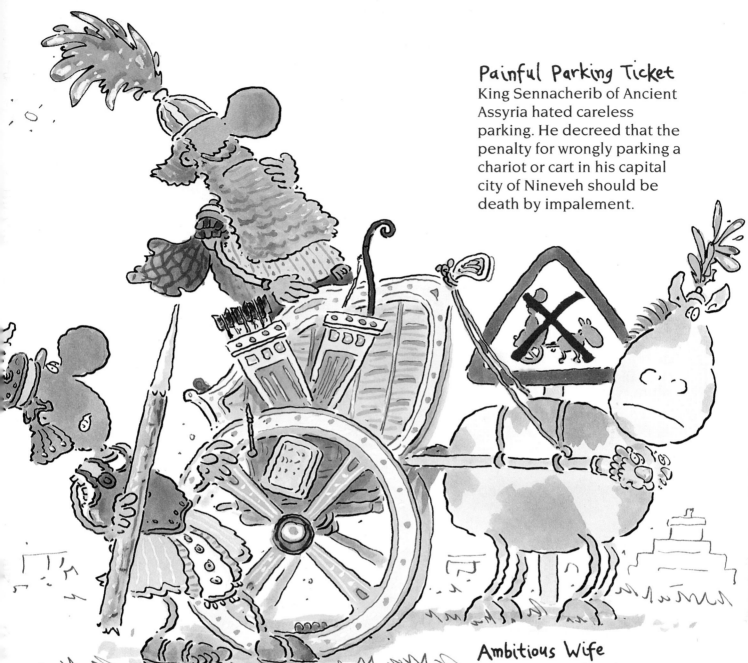

Painful Parking Ticket

King Sennacherib of Ancient Assyria hated careless parking. He decreed that the penalty for wrongly parking a chariot or cart in his capital city of Nineveh should be death by impalement.

Ambitious Wife

Queen Supayalat of nineteenth-century Burma wanted to make sure that her husband's claim to the throne would never be challenged by any of his relatives. Unfortunately, he had rather a lot of them. The Queen arranged a three day feast for 100 of the relatives. While loud music was played to drown their screams, she ordered them to be clubbed to death.

Keep your Hair On

Scalping as a means of proving that a foe had been killed was first used by the Scythians in the fifth century BC. It is doubtful that the American Indians scalped their enemies until told to do so by Europeans. French and British officials paid Indians a bounty for each scalp they produced.

Killer Tortoise

In 1981 in Kenya a tortoise was accused of murdering six people by witchcraft. Tribal elders ordered the creature to be executed but no one was brave enough to carry out the sentence. It was chained to a tree instead. It was later freed while the government made an official inquiry into the incident.

Did You Know....

. . . that there were over 200 crimes in England in 1750 which carried the death penalty. Among them were impersonating a Chelsea Pensioner and digging up trees on Downing Street?

. . . that some of the gladiators in Ancient Rome were women?

. . . that the Roman Emperor Commodus fought in the arena on about 700 occasions and is said to have killed thousands of wild animals?

. . . that 5,000 years ago in Ancient Mesopotamia people did math problems that you can't solve? Try this one – "I dug a square hole and removed one musaru and a half of earth. How deep was the hole?" To solve it you will need to know all about reciprocal numbers and cube roots, and be able to recite your 30 times table!

. . . that the leader of the Spanish Armada, the Duke of Medina Sidonia, had never been to sea before and was horribly seasick for most of the voyage?

. . . that an old cure for seasickness was to swallow a lump of raw pig's fat on a piece of string and then pull it up again?

. . . that many people believe that having a haircut reduces a person's physical strength, just like in the story of Samson? Fijiian chiefs, for instance, were so fearful of being weakened by the barber that they used to eat a man before having a haircut!

. . . that Mongol law forbade washing in running water during a thunderstorm?

. . . that the Mongols used explosive arrows?

. . . that in Peter the Great's Russia there were torture societies whose members tortured each other so they would become immune from this treatment?

. . . that Peter the Great was very fond of dwarfs and kept large numbers of them at his court?

. . . that Charles XII of Sweden loved danger so much that he hunted bears armed only with a pitchfork?

. . . that among the strangest book titles are:

> The Urine Dance of the Zuni Indians of New Mexico
> Stray Leaves from Japanese Papers (which had 400 blank pages of the softest antiseptic paper for emergency use by the desperate traveller)
> A Treatise on Madness by William Battie?

. . . that nicknames for crimes in the eighteenth century included hoisting, sneaking, clouting and dubbing, fam-laying, and buttock twanging?

. . . that Henry Ford once said "History is bunk!"? You probably did. But did you know that he also said "Exercise is bunk. If you are healthy, you don't need it: if you are sick you shouldn't take it"?

. . . that in the eighteenth century people used to pay a small fee to watch the antics of the lunatics in the Bedlam asylum?

. . . that the well-known eccentric, John Mytton, born in 1798 once set fire to his own nightshirt to 'scare away' the hiccups?

. . . that during the siege of Paris, in 1870, the animals in the Paris zoo were slaughtered and eaten. The only survivors were the lions and tigers, who were thought too dangerous to kill; the monkeys because they looked too human; and the hippopotamus whose vast bulk was priced at 80,000 francs, which no one could afford!

. . . that all Egyptian pharaohs, including women, wore false beards?

. . . that the Xhosa people of South Africa slaughtered all their cattle and stopped planting grain in 1856 in the belief that by doing this they could raise their dead warriors and sweep the Europeans from their lands? The actual result was famine.

. . . that the Ottoman Sultan Abdul Aziz so greatly feared being poisoned that for a time he ate only boiled eggs which were cooked by his mother and wrapped in a parcel of black crepe sealed with her personal seal?

. . . that the Emperor Wu of China probably died by drinking an elixir for long life which was prepared by Taoist monks, and contained mercury and arsenic?

. . . that to make sure that candidates in examinations for the Chinese civil service in the Han dynasty did not cheat, they had to choose their questions by firing an arrow at the question paper and then answering the problem which was written nearest to the arrow hole?

. . . that in Ancient China words which contained the name of the emperor or his ancestors could not be spoken by ordinary people, and that writing them down was a very serious offence?

. . . that in Ancient China everyone had to run while moving in the presence of the emperor?

. . . that the Fourth Earl of Sandwich did not invent the sandwich, since this snack was eaten in Ancient Rome?

. . . that people used to believe that scrofula (a form of tuberculosis) or the "king's evil" could be cured by the royal touch? And that Charles II was reported to have touched 92,107 people affected by the disease?

Index